Tchaikowsky Swan Lake Variation

Vivan & Ketan Bhatti

Score

BOSWORTH

Composed for Esther Abrami and recorded by Esther Abrami and
Iyad Sughayer for Sony Classical.

Duration: c. 3 minutes

Order number: BOE100857

Tchaikowsky Swan Lake Variation

(for Violin and Piano after *Scene Moderato, Op. 20*)

Vivan & Ketan Bhatti

Tchaikowsky Swan Lake Variation

Vivan & Ketan Bhatti

Violin Part

BOSWORTH

Tchaikowsky Swan Lake Variation

(for Violin and Piano after *Scene Moderato, Op. 20*)

Vivan & Ketan Bhatti

presto possible

molto rit.

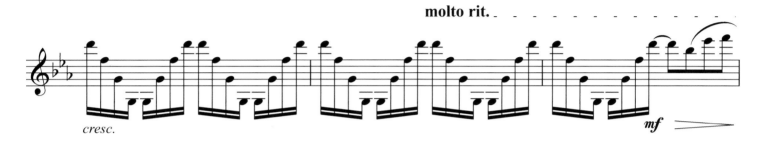

cresc.   *mf*

D A tempo

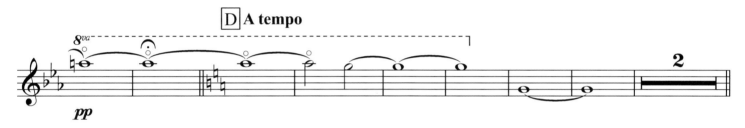

pp   **2**

A1

p

pp

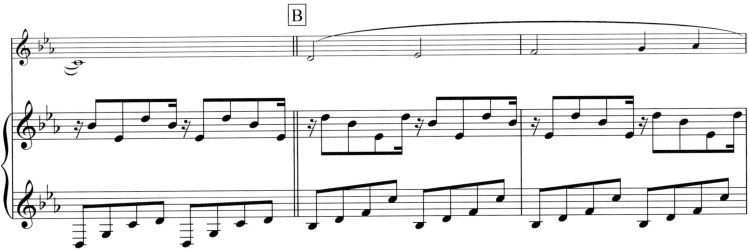

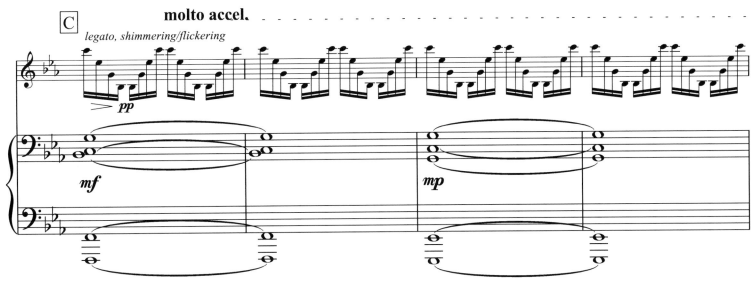

presto possible

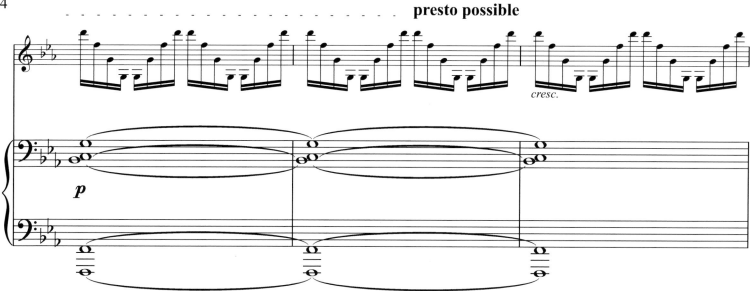

cresc.

molto rit. - - - - - - - - - - - - - - -

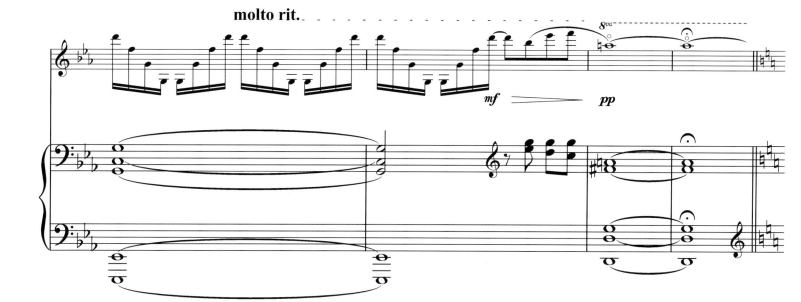

mf ⟩ *pp*

D **A tempo**

pp

A1